Morkie

A Morkie Dog Owner's Guide

Morkie breeding, where to buy, types, care, temperament, cost, health, grooming, diet, and much more included!

By: Lolly Brown

Copyrights and Trademarks

Disclaimer and Legal Notice

Foreword

The Morkie is one of the many designer breed dogs growing in popularity today - and the Morkie has certainly caught the attention of many prospective dog owners for its unique and adorable look, its friendly and amiable temperament, and its fairly low maintenance lifestyle needs.

If you are the owner of a Morkie, or are considering adding a Morkie to your family, you will find some useful information in this book to guide you as you settle down to co-existence with your new family member. Ultimately, though, you should pay attention to your Morkie - they will be the best ones to teach you about their unique and individual needs, quirks, and characteristics.

Table of Contents

Introduction

The Morkie - a.k.a. the Maltiyork, Malkie, Yorkiemalt, Yortese, or Yorktese - is one of the many designer crossbreeds growing in popularity today. The Morkie is a combination of two purebreds: the Maltese and the Yorkshire Terrier, both small dogs, and both unique in temperament, appearance, and characteristics.

It has yet to be seen with any definitive conclusion what the Morkie is truly like - the development of this breed is still fairly recent, and our knowledge still too tentative. Given this short disclaimer, there are some things that have become fairly standard of our knowledge of Morkies, which are presented in the rest of the pages of this book. For the most part, breeders and owners tend to look back to the Maltese and the Yorkie to fill in any gaps in our information of Morkies.

We have sought to compile in this book some of the more generally accepted information regarding Morkies: including grooming, exercise, diet, and their peculiar health conditions. And given the current raging debates on whether it is advisable or not to create crossbreed designer breeds in the first place, we have included a section in the chapter on breeding dogs some food for thought on the advantages and disadvantages of crossbreeding.

Regardless of where you stand on this issue, however, Morkies have been born, and, it seems, will continue to be born in the coming years. Outside of the fad of owning designer dogs - this is simply another breed requiring proper care, attention, and resposible pet ownership from prospective Morkie owners.

Glossary of Dog Terms

AKC – American Kennel Club, the largest purebred dog registry in the United States

Almond Eye – Referring to an elongated eye shape rather than a rounded shape

Apple Head – A round-shaped skull

Balance – A show term referring to all of the parts of the dog, both moving and standing, which produce a harmonious image

Beard – Long, thick hair on the dog's underjaw

Best in Show – An award given to the only undefeated dog left standing at the end of judging

Bitch – A female dog

Bite – The position of the upper and lower teeth when the dog's jaws are closed; positions include level, undershot, scissors, or overshot

Blaze – A white stripe running down the center of the face between the eyes

Board – To house, feed, and care for a dog for a fee

Breed – A domestic race of dogs having a common gene pool and characterized appearance/function

Breed Standard – A published document describing the look, movement, and behavior of the perfect specimen of a particular breed

Buff – An off-white to gold coloring

Clip – A method of trimming the coat in some breeds

Coat – The hair covering of a dog; some breeds have two coats, and outer coat and undercoat; also known as a double coat. Examples of breeds with double coats include German Shepherd, Siberian Husky, Akita, etc.

Condition – The health of the dog as shown by its skin, coat, behavior, and general appearance

Crate – A container used to house and transport dogs; also called a cage or kennel

Crossbreed (Hybrid) – A dog having a sire and dam of two different breeds; cannot be registered with the AKC

Dam (bitch) – The female parent of a dog;

Dock – To shorten the tail of a dog by surgically removing the end part of the tail.

Double Coat – Having an outer weather-resistant coat and a soft, waterproof coat for warmth; see above.

Drop Ear – An ear in which the tip of the ear folds over and hangs down; not prick or erect

Entropion – A genetic disorder resulting in the upper or lower eyelid turning in

Fancier – A person who is especially interested in a particular breed or dog sport

Fawn – A red-yellow hue of brown

Feathering – A long fringe of hair on the ears, tail, legs, or body of a dog

Groom – To brush, trim, comb or otherwise make a dog's coat neat in appearance

Heel – To command a dog to stay close by its owner's side

Hip Dysplasia – A condition characterized by the abnormal formation of the hip joint

Inbreeding – The breeding of two closely related dogs of one breed

Kennel – A building or enclosure where dogs are kept

Litter – A group of puppies born at one time

Markings – A contrasting color or pattern on a dog's coat

Mask – Dark shading on the dog's foreface

Mate – To breed a dog and a bitch

Neuter – To castrate a male dog or spay a female dog

Pads – The tough, shock-absorbent skin on the bottom of a dog's foot

Parti-Color – A coloration of a dog's coat consisting of two or more definite, well-broken colors; one of the colors must be white

Pedigree – The written record of a dog's genealogy going back three generations or more

Pied – A coloration on a dog consisting of patches of white and another color

Prick Ear – Ear that is carried erect, usually pointed at the tip of the ear

Puppy – A dog under 12 months of age

Purebred – A dog whose sire and dam belong to the same breed and who are of unmixed descent

Saddle – Colored markings in the shape of a saddle over the back; colors may vary

Shedding – The natural process whereby old hair falls off the dog's body as it is replaced by new hair growth.

Sire – The male parent of a dog

Smooth Coat – Short hair that is close-lying

Spay – The surgery to remove a female dog's ovaries, rendering her incapable of breeding

Trim – To groom a dog's coat by plucking or clipping

Undercoat – The soft, short coat typically concealed by a longer outer coat

Wean – The process through which puppies transition from subsisting on their mother's milk to eating solid food

Whelping – The act of birthing a litter of puppies

Chapter One: Understanding Morkie Dogs

Nobody can really say they "know" a dog, but there are some standard information regarding Morkies that can guide prospective owners as they care for and raise their Morkies.

Much of what we know is fairly recent - some might say untested, as of yet. Given that this breed is not yet recognized by official kennel clubs such as the AKC, there are no official standards to guide us as to the peculiar nature, temperament and characteristics of this breed. There are similarities that have been apparent, however, such as a gentle and playful temperament, and a certain attachment to their owners which makes them averse to being solitary for long periods of time.

It seems also that the unique pedigree of the Morkie from two different toy breeds have made for a fragile and delicate dog that should not be exposed to rough games and activities. And like its original parents, they also do require more than their fair share of grooming needs.

That said, the Morkie is a friendly, amiable and cheerful dog that does not require much space or much exercise. For some folks, this may be the perfect dog to suit their lifestyle!

Summary of Morkie Facts

Pedigree: Maltese, Yorkshire Terrier

AKC Group: not applicable

Types: not applicable

Breed Size: small

Height: 6 - 8 inches

Weight: 4 - 12 lbs.

Coat Length and Texture: Long and soft, fine and straight

Color: black, brown, tan or white

Appearance: Not standard

Temperament: active and playful, quite needy and form strong attachments to their owners; they can be excitable, energetic, and loyal, with a streak of stubbornness

Strangers: suspicious of strangers and will bark to alert of unusual sounds

Other Dogs: normally friendly with other dogs they have been brought up with

Other Pets: normally friendly with other pets that they have been brought up with

Training: intelligent and smart, but can be difficult; training should begin as early as possible

Exercise Needs: moderate; a few short walks each day with occasional play time

Health Conditions: eye, ear and oral regions: collapsed trachea, reverse sneezing, tracheal collapse, cataracts, medial patellar luxation, hydrocephalus, chronic valvular heart disease, kidney failure, glaucoma

Lifespan: average 10 to 13 years

Morkie Breed History

There does not seem to be any detailed or clear information regarding the origins of the Morkie, aside from some very general information. What is certain is that the Morkie was first bred in the United States, following the recent trend for designer dogs.

Designer dogs are crossbreeds resulting from the intentional breeding of two purebreds in an effort to produce a new dog breed - hopefully one that retains certain desired characteristics of both parents. In the case of the Morkie, this relatively new breed's origins are apparent from the play on their very name: Morkie being a combination of Maltese and Yorkie, the latter being a shorter name for the Yorkshire Terrier. But this little breed can sometimes go under other names, such as Maltiyork, Malkie, Yorkiemalt, Yortese, or Yorktese.

Like most designer dogs of the 20th century, one of the main intentions on the crossbreeding of two purebreds is their appearance - as opposed to crossbreed working dogs who are not referred to by a portmanteau of the parents' names. One might say that designer dogs are mainly motivated by current fashion trends - which would also account for their higher costs. On the other hand, some breeders undertake crossbreeding with the intention of eliminating some of the hereditary or genetic problems or disorders in both breeds. In this case, careful and selective crossbreeding to expand the gene pool is hoped to do precisely that - to breed out some of the more debilitating and fatal canine diseases.

For the Morkie, its popularity seems to stem from its small size, a non-shedding coat, and an interesting "look." Given the breed's recent development, however, most Morkies are still quite varied in appearance and temperament. Some lean closer to a Maltese look, while others favor their Yorkshire Terrier's genes. Their temperaments can also vary from being calm and gentle to active and restless.

The AKC has yet to recognize the Morkie as a registered breed, though enthusiasts are certainly pushing for its recognition as an accepted breed. The difficulty, of course, is that recognition implies a Breed Standard, and given the current variations in appearance and temperament of this modern breed, there has yet to be a determined "standard." It is expected that breed recognition will come only after years of careful and selective breeding, when the breed's unique characteristics and traits have become more uniform, and after the breed itself has grown enough in population as to become distinctive and recognizable.

That said, the Morkie is a recognized breed by the International Designer Canine Registry (IDCR) and the Designer Breed Registry (DBR).

Chapter Two: Things to Know Before Getting a Morkie

This chapter contains some of the more practical information you would need to know before getting a Morkie - things you would have to consider in making sure that a Morkie is right for you and your lifestyle. These cute and adorable little dogs might capture your heart at first sight, but remember that they will live for a long time - a Morkie's lifespan is, on the average, about 10 to 13 years.

Part of responsible pet ownership is making sure that you have the capacity to give a Morkie the kind of care and attention that it needs to live a long and healthy life.

Do You Need a License?

Not all states require dog owners to have a license, and a simple enquiry will tell you whether your local laws mandate you to get a license for your Morkie. Whether or not you are legally obligated to register and get a license for your dog, it is always a good idea to do so voluntarily. The requirements for getting a dog license can be checked with your local city council.

The reason behind getting a dog license is usually proper identification - so regardless of the differences in licensing requirements between states, the essence is usually the same: they will issue you a dog tag with proper identification of the dog and the owner, as well as the appropriate contact numbers. This is usually given after the payment of an appropriate fee, and proof of rabies vaccination. So in addition to being able to trace the dog back to you in case he ever gets lost, licensing is also intended to safeguard the public by making sure that dogs are properly vaccinated against rabies.

Rabies shots are valid for a year, after which they need to be renewed. This is also the reason why dog licenses are only valid for a year. Once they expire, in order to renew, you will again have to show proof of the most recent rabies vaccination.

Morkies are not usually wanderers - they prefer to stick close to their owners. And being toy breeds that can live pretty happily inside your home, you might think that the dangers of you losing your Morkie is pretty nil. But one can never be sure about these things, and it is always better to be prepared. All dogs may tend to wander at one point or another during their lifetime, and that would certainly include the Morkie. Make sure he can find his way back home to you as quickly as possible by getting the appropriate license and identification tags.

How Many Morkie Dogs Should You Keep?

You can certainly keep more than one Morkie if you are confident that you can care for them in the way they need to be cared for. And keeping a dog is certainly not cheap, so make sure that this is something you can afford to do. Aside from the dog food and their grooming needs - the latter being quite extensive for Morkies - you will also be shouldering their medical costs and veterinarian bills. And twice the Morkie means twice the energy spent on their care, exercise, training, and housebreaking. As stated above - you can certainly get more than one Morkie if you are confident that you can handle it. Just make sure that you know what you are getting into first.

These basic questions of care and proper attention really should come first over the more common reason people have for getting more than one dog - which is to give their other dog company. If you care for and raise a Morkie right, the only company he will really need is yours.

You should also consider that having more than one dog in the house means that you will be dividing your time and attention between them, which means less care than if it were only one dog. It is also possible that these two dogs might not like each other - or, once they grow up and are sexually mature, they might begin growing crazy whenever the female is in heat. Two dogs can easily multiply into a new litter of puppies. This is not necessarily a bad thing - but if it means that you will not be able to give each individual Morkie the care and attention that they need, then you really must reconsider. First make sure that you know what goes into the care of one Morkie, and that you are fully capable of providing it - before getting another one.

Do Morkie Dogs Get Along with Other Pets?

Morkies are generally even-tempered, kind, and friendly. Providing they have been properly socialized, and providing that they are getting proper care, attention, food and exercise - they will be mild-mannered and will likely become fast friends with your other household pets.

That said, exercising a little caution is also a good idea. Make the proper introductions between your family members and the Morkie, and the Morkie and the other pets in the house with whom he will be living alongside with. These introductions should, of course, be properly supervised in case there are any aggressive displays on either side. Be observant during the first few days to make sure that everything is going smoothly.

It is also a good idea to factor in the individual personalities of your pets before actually getting a Morkie. Morkies will be pretty demanding in their need for attention, and while friendly, they might have moments of excitability and high energy barking. Then consider your other pets in the house and whether their temperaments suit each other well.

How Much Does it Cost to Keep a Morkie?

Bear in mind the your cost for keeping a Morkie will necessarily be higher during the first year. This is because you will have to factor in some initial expenses such as the purchase price of the Morkie itself, veterinary examinations, and the purchase of various tools and equipment such as their crate, spaying or neutering when desired, grooming tools, and various other pet accessories such as toys, a collar and a leash.

Expect to spend upwards of $1,000 during your first year - probably more depending on where you decide to purchase your Morkie. If you adopt one from a rescue or a shelter, you will probably shell out an average of about $150-250, whereas if you get a Morkie directly from a breeder who can provide you with proper papers of the purebred parents, and a complete array of medical and health checks, these little designer dogs can cost an average of $1,000 to $2,500 - way more than the usual cost for purebred dogs. This greater expense seems to be purely on account of their current popularity and the raging celebrity fashion trends among dog owners.

On the darker side, this sudden boom of high demand for designer dogs has also resulted in widespread backyard puppy farms and breeders who are only in it for the money, regardless of the health and wellbeing of this crossbreed. So prospective Morkie owners are advised to exercise due caution in deciding where to purchase their Morkies.

Aside from the purchase price, here is an average estimate of some of the initial costs of keeping one Morkie:

Initial Costs of Keeping a Morkie	
Spaying or Neutering	$200
Medical Exam	$70
Crate	$95
Training	$110
Toys and Treats	$55
Food/Water Bowl	$20
Miscellaneous Accessories	$50

This initial breakdown does not yet factor in the annual and recurring costs of keeping a dog, which includes the annual checkups, dog food, grooming and licensing costs. Below is a table showing an average estimate of these annual costs, which you will have to add to the initial costs for the first year:

Annual Expenses for Keeping a Morkie	
Dog Food	$120
Annual Medical Exams	$235

License	$15
Pet Health Insurance	$225
Grooming Costs	$200
Miscellaneous Yearly Expenses	$45
Total	840

These are just average estimates, of course, and can considerably be higher or lower depending on various other factors. Some experts do recommend, however, that if you d not get pet health insurance, you might at least set aside $1,000 - 2,000 for unforeseen medical emergencies and pet health costs.

What are the Pros and Cons of Morkie Dogs?

Here is a basic overview of some of the pros and cons of the Morkie breed, and can give you a quick assessment of what Morkie ownership entails, and whether or not this is really the right breed for you:

Pros for the Morkie Breed
- This little fellow does not require much in terms of space and exercise. A Morkie can live happily in an

apartment and with short daily walks each day and the occasional fetching games.

- This is an affectionate, friendly and cheerful breed, so you probably won't have much problems with aggression or hostility. There won't be any trouble with a Morkie getting along with kids and other pets of the family.

- What makes the Morkies popular is their unique appearance and gentle temperament. This dog was bred to be lapdogs, and they certainly look adorable and cute. If this is the type of dog you are looking for, then a Morkie may be the perfect choice for you!

Cons for the Morkie Breed

- This is a needy breed, and will not like to be left alone for long periods of time. If your lifestyle keeps you out of the house for most of the day, then this breed is probably not the best one for you.

- This is a high maintenance breed when it comes to grooming. It has a long growing coat that needs constant care and regular brushing, or he might end up with matted and tangled hair which can be painful and would eventually require the services of a professional groomer

- This is a fragile and delicate breed, so you might want to exercise caution and supervision when it comes to games and exercises.

- Given that this is a relatively new breed, there isn't much yet that is truly known about it - including its possible health conditions and temperament, which can still be pretty variable. Neither is it recognized by official kennel clubs like the AKC so there is a bit of risk in keeping a Morkie - mostly because of all the unknowns about this breed.

Chapter Three: Purchasing Your Morkie

If you have decided that a Morkie is the right dog for you, it is time to start thinking about where a good place would be to get a Morkie. But despite the recent popularity of designer dogs such as the Morkie, it is not always easy to find a good and reputable breeder. Designer dogs cost more than purebreds, and because of this, there have been a proliferation of backyard breeders who are only in it for the money. As a result, there have also been an increase in the number of stray, abandoned and unwanted crossbreeds with no home to go to. You might, therefore, look into the possibility of adopting rescued Morkies first.

Adopting Morkies Needing Good Homes

One good thing about adopting rescues is that they certainly cost less - and you will have the satisfaction of knowing that one homeless dog has found a good home with a good owner. Besides, even buying a high-priced Morkie from a breeder is no guarantee that they will be healthier than a resilient Morkie that has survived worse conditions. There is no such thing as a 100% health guarantee in breeding dogs, and a breeder who tells you that is certainly lying.

So check out your local rescues first. Since this is a new breed, you will probably find them among other rescued breeds. Chances are you will find a number of Morkies in rescue centers given recent efforts to stamp out puppy mills. And don't be afraid to ask questions, such as where the Morkie came from, how it came to be in the rescue, and where the adoption fee goes to. Ask about any health examinations given the dog, and how their behavior has been so far.

If you are unsure about where to find the local rescue nearest your area, the AKC carries a listing of rescues on their site, organized as the AKC Rescue Network. You can at least be sure that these are reputable dog shelters and rescues, and are not puppy mills masquerading as rescues. The fact of it is that some breeders will be unscrupulous enough to try to make a market of breeding dogs, regardless of whether or not adhere to reputable breeding practices. Be discerning as you check out your options.

How to Choose a Reputable Morkie Breeder

One of the main difficulties in choosing a reputable Morkie breeder is that you cannot rely on listings of organizations like the AKC to screen breeders for a breed that they do not recognize in the first place. If you are willing to shell out the greater expense for a Morkie puppy, it pays to be able to determine whether you are dealing with a good and reputable breeder in the first place.

The first thing you should consider is that a reputable breeder will be very particular about the puppy's health. How do they do this? They make sure, first and foremost, that they are breeding from purebreds that have gone through proper health screening and health checks. They should be able to show you registration papers for the purebred parents. They should also be able to show you medical papers clearing them of some of the more common genetic illnesses to which the parents are prone to. But most of all, they should be able to frankly discuss with you the risks and benefits of crossbreeding.

Regardless of whether or not crossbreeding for designer dogs is a good idea or not, good breeders will be very particular about the care that goes into the breeding process itself. Ask to see the site where the puppies and the mother are kept. It should be clean, and the puppies and their mother should look healthy and well-fed. Don't hesitate to ask questions about how the breeding and the whelping went: was it an easy delivery? Is this the dam's first litter? The stud's? Is this the first Morkie litter the breeder has produced? If not, how did the previous litters turn out, and did they come from the same parents? Ask questions about how the mother and the puppies are doing, how they are feeding, and how energetic they are.

But best of all, perhaps, you should ask the breeder why he or she is breeding Morkies. Given the current raging debates for and against the breeding of designer dogs, it may not be easy to decide which side is right or wrong. And while you certainly cannot dictate to others which are good reasons or not, you will at least be able to tell from the breeder's intentions how much care he has actually put in into the breeding of this litter of Morkie puppies. After all, the greater expense of designer dogs like the Morkie does warrant that extra special care to the breed - quite aside from the Morkie's unique and charming looks.

Tips for Selecting a Healthy Morkie Puppy

When you finally do get that call from the breeder of your choice that the puppies are ready, you may be wondering what to look out for in a puppy to make sure that it is in good health. Here are a few tips and guidelines to help you:

- A good foundation must already have been laid for proper socialization. This means that the puppy must demonstrate a natural curiosity about you, and should also demonstrate the trademark friendliness of the breed. If the puppy is too shy, timid, nervous, fearful, or even outright aggressive, this means that the puppies haven't been handled much - demonstrating, perhaps, that the breeder hasn't been taking as good care of the litter as you thought.
- Watch out for telling signs of a dirty litterbox and unhealthy-looking discharges from the eyes or nose. A healthy puppy should also be moving around happily. You should certainly think twice if a puppy isn't moving around at all, or sitting or lying down in what seems like an unhealthy or unnatural manner.
- Look out for potential behavioral problems such as too much aggressiveness, chewing at things, and pushing others out of the way. Remember that this little fellow will become a part of your family for the

next few years, and you will be dealing with him on a daily basis. Those bold, daring displays might endear you to him at first, but think about having to deal with that kind of behavior every day! Besides, Morkies are, while playful, a cheerful, kind and gentle breed. If you are looking for Morkies specifically for these qualities, then pick the Morkie puppy that displays the precise temperament you are looking for, and which will suit your own lifestyle.

- The puppy should be responsive to environmental stimuli. Your presence, your voice, your smell - these must arouse his curiosity. If it doesn't, and you find yourself dealing with an unnaturally passive puppy, you might think twice about the puppy's health and socialization skills.

Chapter Four: Caring for Your New Morkie

Now that you've brought your Morkie home, it is time for you to settle in and get to know each other.

One of the things that most people like about Morkies is that they do not require much room - in terms of living space and even exercise requirements - they can be considered low maintenance. A Morkie is, therefore, a good choice for people who want to have dogs but do not have the space to accommodate larger dogs who require a fenced-in yard. Morkies and other toy dog breeds make it possible for dog lovers living in apartments to add a dog to their family.

A Morkie is generally not a yappy or noisy dog. They are a calm, gentle breed whose needs are pretty basic: a regular diet of nutritious food, moderate exercise, and your company and attention. They can be pretty needy, and are happy if you are near. This is not a dog that you can leave alone for long periods of time. If you are working long hours, for instance, and would need to leave your Morkie at home for most of the day, this breed is probably not the right one for you - either to groom them (which you would need to do on a daily basis, at least for regular brushing and combing), or just to laze around with.

Ideal Habitat Requirements for your Morkie

Once you bring your Morkie home, you will certainly need to adjust your lifestyle to factor him in, just as he will also need to adjust to living with you. And one of the things that you might wonder about is your Morkie's sleeping arrangements. If he lazes around on the couch and on the bed during the day, is it a good idea to let him sleep there at night?

Ultimately, this is a question that each owner will have to answer for himself or herself. Be aware, though, that allowing your Morkie to sleep in your bed with you does raise some safety questions.

A number of possibilties arise: what if you roll over during the night and unknowingly roll over your Morkie? What if your Morkie rolls in his sleep and rolls right out of bed and onto the floor? This is a delicate breed, and it might not take much to cause him injury.

Besides, a habit such as this that is built early on in a Morkie's life may be impossible to break as he grows older. Are you really willing to share your bed with your Morkie indefinitely? This may not be a problem for single people who do not share their bed with anyone - but what about once they get married? Or have kids who like to jump on beds? If they have gotten used to sleeping in the bed with you, they might have a difficult time understanding why you are suddenly demoting them to a box on the floor, or confining them to a crate in the kitchen at night. Ultimately, it's probably best to consider what would be workable for you and your lifestyle for the long term.

Again, the choice is entirely up to you. Though some discipline in the beginning will probably end up saving you a lot of frustration in the long run.

Exercise Requirements for Morkie Dogs

Like most tiny breeds, the Morkie is a fairly high energy dog. And yet they will not need too much exercise, either. This is because their energy consumption is also fairly high. A short, daily walk once or twice a day for about 20 to 30 minutes each day can be sufficient. If he is still energetic and restless after these walks, you can probably shake things up with games such as fetching, for instance, or by increasing the length of their walk. As with any dog, insufficient exercise can lead to destructive behavior.

While Morkies are good with children, you should make sure that they are not exposed to too much rough housing because they will injure quite easily. If you do have children in the house, it is probably best to teach them early on the boundaries with playing with the Morkie - for the safety of all. It is probably best for these play sessions to be supervised affairs.

That said, Morkies love the company of his human family, and his natural playfulness means that he will also enjoy games and playing with his owners. If you do take him out for a walk, make sure that he is properly leashed and that he has his ID tags on his collar.

Consult with your veterinarian at first as to the proper exercise requirements for your Morkie. Thereafter, simply pay attention to your dog's daily state. If he is too energetic when you come home, he probably needs more exercise. If he is too tired, he probably needs less. If he seems bored, then you probably just need to shake things up a bit with some variety and games that will appeal to his playful, and oftentimes silly, nature.

Chapter Five: Meeting Your Morkie's Nutritional Needs

As with most dogs, a good and balanced diet and nutrition is the cornerstone of a Morkie's good health. It may be tempting to overfeed Morkies those little treats throughout the day, but it is important that you keep him on a regular feeding schedule of healthy dog food each day. Not only will this help you in housebreaking your little Morkie, but good feeding and nutrition can prolong his life and keep him healthy and fit.

The Nutritional Needs of Dogs

Just as it is with human diet, balanced canine nutrition depends on your dog being able to get all the essential nutrients he needs on a daily basis. These would provide him with energy, support cellular growth and metabolism, and boost his immunity. The following are the basic nutrients that dogs need, including a short description of each:

Proteins

Mainly obtained from meat and most meat-based products, protein is essential for growth and cellular regeneration and repair, and for Morkies, are necessary to help maintain their beautiful long and silky coat. Be aware that experts do not recommend feeding your dog raw eggs, as this may have actually be harmful to their health.

Carbohydrates

This is usually derived from fiber-based products, and help in maintaining the intestinal health of your pet. Some carbohydrates can even be a good source of energy for your pet.

Fats

Fats provide your pet with a concentrated source of energy, and are also essential for some vitamins (A, E, D and

K) to be absorbed. They help in protecting the internal organs and are vital in cellular production.

Vitamins and Minerals

Vitamins and minerals usually cannot be synthesized by a dog's body, so the primary source of these are the synthesized versions obtainable in commercially available quality dog foods. Vitamins and minerals help in the normal functioning of their bodies, and also helps maintain their bones and teeth.

Water

Water must, of course, not be forgotten. Just like humans, about 60 to 70 percent of a dog's body weight is comprised of water, and he will have to replenish this often as he loses it. Clean water must always be available to your Morkie; loss of water in the body can certainly cause illness, and severe dehydration can be fatal.

How to Select a High-Quality Dog Food Brand

Not all dog food are made the same. But how do you know which dog food are of better quality compared to others? Is cost a reliable measure of better quality?

The first thing you should probably do is ask your veterinarian what dog food he recommends for your Morkie.

And don't stop there. Ask other dog owners - preferably Morkie owners. Research, read a lot, and ask questions.

You might also begin by learning to read the label. First of all, check for a nutritional adequacy statement for the AAFCO, or the Association of American Feed Control Officials. If you find this, you can at least be assured that a particular dog food meets the minimum nutritional requirements. As to content, most experts agree that meat-based dog food is better for dogs, and in place of providing them meat diets, meat-based dog food is probably the next best thing. Some may claim that a vegetable diet is good for humans, but the same cannot be said for canines who do need some meat in their diet. They are omnivores - which means they can eat both meat and plant-based food, but no one will seriously contend that dogs in the wild will always choose plants over meat!

How can you tell if a particular brand of dog food is meat-based? You can usually tell from the label. The first five ingredients will tell you whether a particular dog food is meat-based or not - such as chicken, beef, turkey, or lamb. Avoid grains since their stomach cannot digest grains. Also steer clear of corn, soy, and any by-products. Steer clear of aritificial flavors and colors, as well as preservatives.

And most importantly, you should stick to small breed dog food as these are prepared in tiny portions that are more suitable to a small dog's digestive capacity.

Yes, it can be confusing at first - especially given the many available choices of commercial dog food now available, and all the things you have to look for and avoid. Do your research, ask around, but most importantly - pay attention to how your Morkie responds to the dog food diet you are providing him.

Tips for Feeding Your Morkie

Your Morkie's feeding schedule will certainly have to follow your lifestyle to some extent. And while some owners stick to a twice-a-day feeding schedule, there are those who worry whether or not their Morkie is getting the proper nutrients since toy breeds do tend to be nibblers. Some owners handle this by free feeding, or making food available throughout the day. But this kind of feeding could make housebreaking more difficult. So what to do?

It might be a good idea to feed 4 to 6 times a day to begin with, in smaller portions, at regular intervals. Little by little, you can adjust your Morkie's feeding schedule until you can settle on twice or thrice a day, depending on your availability. During this time, you should probably limit the treats you give him, as it is more important to get him used to regular meals at fixed schedules to ensure that he gets his proper daily nutrient requirements.

Remember to feed in proper portions according to his age requirement. You would not feed a puppy the same way as you would a mature Morkie, or even a senior Morkie, despite the fact that this breed never does seem to grow out of puppyhood. It is natural for some dogs, particularly tiny breeds, to be a little finicky now and then - especially as they age. You can probably shake things up by varying the food you give them from time to time, though you should always make it a point to give them quality dog food as much as possible - tiny breeds will not really do well when you skimp them on their food.

Consult with your veterinarian regarding the proper portions best for your Morkie - this will usually be dependent on his weight, his age, and his lifestyle. More active dogs require more food than sedentary ones. You will probably also hear something about a dog's RER, or Resting Energy Requirement. This is the basic energetic requirement of a dog which also determines his daily calorie per cup requirement. The RER is determined by a dog's weight, and is arrived at using the following formula, which is used for dogs weighing between 2 and 45 kg (5-99 lbs):

RER = 30 (body weight in kilograms) + 70

But remember that the RER is the daily energy requirement of a dog when he is at rest. Being active in any way - which is the opposite of being at rest - modifies your Morkie's RER. The same is also true if your Morkie begins to go through certain life changes such as adolescence, being spayed or neutered, pregnancy, or growing old.

The following table shows some ways by which the RER is modified due to certain life changes that your Morkie can go through:

Neutered Adult	RER x 1
Intact Adult	RER x 1.6
Moderate Work Adult	RER x 3
Pregnant dog in the last 21 days before birth	RER x 3
Weaning Puppy	RER x 3
Adolescent Puppy	RER x 2
Obese Puppy undergoing weight loss activities	RER x 1

In principle, though, these modifications are really not very difficult to understand. A more active dog requires more food than an inactive dog. Pregnant dogs require more food, just as lactating dogs do. It is not unlike how we humans also increase the portions of our daily diet whenever we are hungry, tired, active, or working. Simply put, we need more food to sustain us as we go through these different activities. The same is also true for your Morkie.

Remember that you can only safely make little adjustments to your dog's daily diet. Before you make any drastic changes, always consult with your veterinarian. But your best gauge is probably your Morkie: if he seems thin and listless, you probably aren't feeding him enough. If he is starting to grow a bit round around the middle, then you're probably feeding him too much. Always use your best judgment.

Dangerous Foods to Avoid

A word of caution should probably be given regarding the feeding of toy dogs. Most days, they are carried around in their owner's laps, and some owners even carry around these designer dogs in their bags or purse. The temptation to hand feed them is, therefore, greater. But not all the food that are edible to us humans are good for dogs. Some can actually be quite toxic. The following is a list of some harmful people food that you should never feed your Morkie. If he does ingest them for some reason, you should call emergency services right away:

- Alcohol
- Apple seeds
- Avocado
- Cherry pits
- Chocolate
- Citrus
- Coconut
- Coffee
- Cooked Bones
- Fat Trimmings
- Garlic
- Grapes/raisins
- Hops
- Macadamia nuts
- Milk and Dairy
- Mold
- Mushrooms
- Mustard seeds
- Onions/leeks
- Peach pits
- Potato leaves/stems
- Raw meat and eggs
- Rhubarb leaves
- Salty snacks
- Tea
- Tomato leaves/stems
- Walnuts
- Wild Mushrooms
- Xylitol
- Yeast dough

On this note, you should probably keep your veterinarian's and the local emergency clinic's numbers handy at all times just in case an unforeseen emergency pops up.

Chapter Six: Training Your Morkie

Given that the Morkie is a relatively new breed, the variations in their coat colors and types, as well as in their appearance, also reflects a variety in their temperament. Generally, though, a Morkie is a gentle and affectionate breed. But when it comes to training a Morkie, you may find some stubborness occasionally mixed in with moderate trainability. Training should really start as early as possible, and it all begins with socialization.

Socializing Your New Morkie Puppy

Socialization is doubly more important for the Morkie puppy as this breed does have a tendency towards timidity and shyness. Most puppies develop a natural caution and suspicion of the strange things around them as they grow older, and if unchecked, can make for a fearful life for the dog as they grow older. Socialization should begin as early as possible. Most experts agree that after 18 weeks, it can be difficult, if not impossible, to socialize puppies. Their natural caution then becomes ingrained, and each new thing can cause timidity, suspicion, fear, and even aggression. Needless to say, this will make for a very stressful life for Morkies living alongside humans in a human environment.

Proper socialization is really not complicated, and neither does it take much. All you really need to do is to expose your new puppy, little by little, to new experiences each day and in a positive atmosphere, just so he understands that there is nothing to fear in the world around him. Begin by getting him accustomed to your presence and the presence of your family, as well as the home environment. Once he has gained a fair amount of confidence in exploring the world around him, you can begin to take him out for short walks each day to explore the neighborhood. Afterwards, you can take him out to the park for some games, where he can get used to the presence of other people and other dogs.

There is really no standard socialization procedure. Be attentive to how your Morkie reacts to things, reassure them when they need it, and try to push them out of their comfort zone little by little until they gain more confidence. Every little exposure to something new - including veterinary checkups and even a visit to the groomers - also builds up on their experience of the world. While you should not rush socialization, it is advisable to expose your Morkie to as much stimulation as he can handle within his first 18 weeks. Never forget, however, that this breed is naturally fragile and delicate, so any rough housing or rough games should probably be avoided.

Housebreaking Your Morkie Puppy

For a relatively new breed, Morkies are already getting some reputation for being difficult to housetrain. Is this an accurate statement, though? Morkies are fairly intelligent, and while they may easily pick up on some of the commands you are teaching them, they can be a bit stubborn when it comes to housebreaking.

And yet some Morkies do respond well to housebreaking training. What makes the difference? It really depends on the dog, and each is individual as all dogs are. Just remember to be patient, consistent, and firm - even if it is for a longer time than you expected. Morkies don't respond well to harsh treatment, so you might explore positive methods such as rewards training instead, using praise or treats to reinforce desired behavior. Explore and experiment with various methods to see which one works best.

Here are a few tips that might guide you as you potty train your Morkie:

- Containment is key. You can keep your Morkie in a crate or within a specific room of the house while he is being housebroken. This limits potential accidents around the house, while at the same time limiting his exposure to various stimuli so that he can have some focus on your housebreaking rules.
- Remember to have a fixed feeding schedule, and a fixed schedule for whenever you take him out for his potty break. Some owners also use bells on the door, teaching the Morkie to ring the bell whenever he needs to be taken outside for his bathroom break. The goal is that he learn to ring the bell whenever he needs to go. Some smart Morkies, however, may actually learn to ring the bell anytime he wants to go outside to play! So be consistent - teach him that the bell should only be rung for regularly scheduled

bathroom breaks. Or you can skip this altogether and just bring him outside at regular intervals.

- If they do have accidents inside the house, don't lose your cool. Just be calm, and take them outside immediately. Praise them if they do go when they are outside, and be firm in your disapproval should they go inside the house or inside the crate. Disapproval does not mean being harsh, however. Remember that the puppy has no idea what you want, and peeing and pooing is, to him, only a natural thing to do. He will eventually learn what you want him to do - just be consistent, be patient, and don't forget to dole out the praises or in voicing your disapproval immediately after the act. Doing so hours later - only when you have found the accident - will only confuse him. At that point, he may be busy with playing, for instance, and he may think that this is what you disapprove of!

- If your Morkie pees and poops a lot even with the regular feeding and bathroom breaks, it just might be physiological! Take him to the vet to make sure that he has no problems in his system that makes him go more often than usual, and be sure that he is getting all his appropriate nutritional needs. It might also be useful to remember that puppies do tend to go a lot - and not so different from human babies or toddlers.

He might just need time to gain better bladder and bowel control as he grows older.

Positive Reinforcement for Obedience Training

Do you really need to *train* Morkies? After all, this little designer dog was bred to be a lapdog, and its main purpose should really just be to sit in your lap and keep you company. As long as they're housebroken and properly socialized, anyone can be pretty satisfied with a Morkie just sitting quietly and looking pretty.

Dogs are an intelligent bunch, and the Morkie is no less so. Whether or not you decide to teach your Morkie tricks and commands is really up to you. It would certainly be helpful to teach them some of the more basic commands, however, such as recognizing their name, and to learn the commands of "Come Here," and "Heel."

Other tricks you can teach them are fetch, roll over, play dead, and "leave it" - for things that you would rather they left alone. These would likely appeal to the sometimes silly and clownish nature of the Morkie, and these training sessions should be enjoyable to the Morkies because all they really want is to be in your company and to have your attention.

How do you go about training your Morkie? Positive Reinforcement is key. This is an affectionate breed, and they will respond well to rewards, treats and praise. On the other hand, brief periods of withdrawal of attention and affection can teach them that certain behavior also meet with your disapproval.

You needn't push it, though. Morkies are pretty content with just curling up in your lap and sleeping anyway. They will need exercise in small doses, just as training can be done daily, also in small doses. The important thing throughout all this is for you and your Morkie to enjoy each other's company.

Chapter Seven: Grooming Your Morkie

This tiny toy breed will have fairly high grooming and maintenance needs. Whether or not the Yorkie or the Maltese coat is more predominant in your Morkie, both parents have long-haired coats that continue to grow throughout their lives and will require constant and regular grooming. As with any long-haired breed, regular brushing is at least necessary to prevent matting or tangles, which can be painful for your dog if left for too long. If for any reason you do skip a day's worth of grooming, you will quickly learn how much more work is left for you the day after.

Avoid this in the first place by brushing your Morkie's coat at least once regularly. If you do not have the time to devote to the regular grooming of your Morkie (or the resources to take them regularly to a professional groomer's), then perhaps this breed - or any other long-haired dog breed - is not the right one for you. A Morkie with matted or tangled hair can be a very sad sight to see.

You might reasonably expect some manifestation of both coat types in any Morkie, so grooming can involve the unique grooming needs of both. Both are long-haired breeds, but while the Maltese coat is cotton-like, that of the Yorkie is more silky in texture. You should be able to adapt your Morkie's grooming needs to his peculiar coat type. Many times, grooming requires care for both varieties.

Recommended Tools to Have on Hand
- slicker brush
- pin brush
- comb
- dog grooming clippers and scissors
- dog ear cleaning equipment
- dog nail trimmers
- high quality dog shampoo and conditioner
- dog toothpaste and toothbrush
- canine eye wipes

Tips for Bathing and Grooming Morkie Dogs

All bathing and grooming should be done in a positive, gentle and reassuring atmosphere so as not to cause unintentional injury and trauma to the little Morkie. This is a fragile breed, and they will certainly not respond well to harsh treatment. It is always best to start them out when they are young - this allows them to get used to regular grooming, which will certainly make it easier for you when they grow up. They might even come to enjoy these grooming sessions, which would undoubtedly make it more pleasurable for you, too.

Bath time for the tiny Morkie can be done once a week, or once every two weeks. The use of high quality dog shampoo and conditioner is necessary for long-haired breeds such as the Morkie because you do want to preserve the natural soft and silky texture of their coat as much as possible. This keeps their coats from losing its natural oils and becoming dry, thus also making the regular brushing and combing much easier and more enjoyable. Rinse thoroughly, then use a towel to dry their coat, running it along their body in long swipes to avoid tangling in the hair. Then you can comb out their hair using a blow dryer at its lowest setting to completely dry them off.

But while you may be able to get away with a weekly or twice-a-week bath, regular brushing is a must! A Morkie's coat is more like hair rather than fur, and because of its length, will certainly tangle or get matted unless combed out and brushed on a regular basis. If your Morkie does develop any difficult tangles or matting in their coat that is difficult or even painful to remove, it is probably advisable for you to bring them to a professional groomer.

This is especially so because Morkies are a pretty fragile breed, and rough handling even during grooming sessions might actually end up hurting or injuring them. Not to mention the pain that comes from matted or tangled fur in the first place. You will, in any case, likely have to bring your Morkie to a groomer anyway - for unless you are very confident that you know what you are doing - the need for clipping or trimming your Morkie's coat is best left to a professional groomer. Trimming the hair growing between the pads of the feet, as well as the hair that grows over and around the eyes and ears are particularly tricky places to be wielding scissors or clippers. A monthly visit to a groomer should be sufficient.

For these daily grooming needs, just remember to brush gently. Use the appropriate tool for the type of coat you are dealing with. This can be the perfect bonding time for you and your Morkie, especially since this breed's temperament does lean towards a certain neediness in attention and socialization. They enjoy being around their owners. Daily grooming sessions done in a positive and playful manner can go a long way to keeping your Morkie physically and mentally happy.

These grooming sessions are also an opportune time for a regular physical examination of your Morkie. Run your hands gently over their delicately-boned body, just to make sure that they are physically healthy and that there are no unexpected lumps or bumps anywhere. This breed also does tend to be teary-eyed given the presence of long hair near or covering their eyes, so using moist wipes to wipe away any unsightly discharge from the corner of their eyes is also recommended. Some owners handle this incidence of tearing of the eyes by simply tying their Morkie's hair back and away from the eyes, or by giving them a trim or cut to open up their field of vision. The choice of which one is better is really up to you - as well as the choice among the many puppy cuts now becoming popular among other toy breeds. Of course, you can certainly opt not to have your Morkie's coat trimmed, but if you do so, you should adhere to daily and even twice a day brushing in order to maintain the beauty of their long coat.

Other Grooming Tasks

Aside from bathing and brushing, grooming also requires attention to the sections below, including trimming the nails, cleaning the ears, and brushing the teeth of your Morkie.

Trimming Your Morkie's Nails

It is probably best that you entrust the trimming of your Morkie's nails to a professional groomer. This is a very tiny and delicate breed, and given that the long hair that grows over the paws might obscure the nails, it is easy to get careless and you just might end up causing unintentional injury. Have the groomer show you how it is done, and once you begin to feel more confident with doing it yourself, you can handle this yourself. But always remember to proceed slowly and gently as you do so.

Cleaning Your Morkie's Ears

The cleaning of a Morkie's ears should not be overlooked. Given the long hair of this tiny breed, especially if its ears flop down like its Maltese progenitor, the retention of moisture inside the ear can make it a breeding ground for bacteria and infection. Air should be able to circulate freely within the ear. If it cannot, you can certainly keep down the chances of an infection by ear cleaning and making sure that it is clean and dry.

But always exercise caution. The inside of a dog's ear is very sensitive, and wrong handling may certainly cause them injury. It is doubly more important to be careful given the Morkie's small size. If you have never cleaned your Morkie's ears before, it is best to have a vet or a professional groomer show you how it's done. When you are confident that you can do this by yourself, make sure you are using the proper tools and equipment. Always proceed cautiously and gently.

Brushing Your Morkie's Teeth

You can use quality dog toothpaste and a good dog toothbrush to clean your Morkie's teeth. But at first, you may wish to begin using only a finger, and only working to reach the front teeth. The goal is to get them used to the feel of a foreign object rubbing against their teeth. Dogs can't spit, and this is why it is important to use dog toothpaste which they can safely swallow.

Eventually, you might be able to reach the back teeth, but there is really no rush. You will want to proceed slowly on this, and again, it should be done in a positive atmosphere for both yourself and your Morkie.

Chapter Eight: Breeding Your Morkie

There is a certain basic principle which reputable breeders adhere to: that one should breed dogs only for the improvement of the breed. On one hand, this means not breeding dogs with any kind of disease or illness, whether congenital or acquired. On the other extreme, it also means breeding dogs with desired characteristics such as size, intelligence, good health, and preferred coat colors in order to preserve these genetic traits and to have them be carried on by the offspring.

But what about crossbreeding?

Proponents of crossbreeding claim that, after all, most if not all of the purebred dogs known today were all the result of crossbreeding at one point or another in the dog's pedigree history. These purebreds are what they are now because breeders of long ago also sought to produce breeds most suited for one job of another: whether hunting, herding, or retrieving. But is it really the same?

There is a growing popularity of designer dogs such as the Morkie - a mix of a Maltese and Yorkshire Terrier. In the same vein as old crossbreeding patterns, two purebreds are mated together in an effort to bring together the parents' desired characteristics in their offsprings. The principles of canine breeding are pretty much the same, and are discussed later on in this chapter. But it might be helpful, first and foremost, to take a closer look at the possible advantages and disadvantages of crossbreeding.]

Breeders everywhere are exhorted to remember that health checks are still important, and that they are still responsible for the puppies born in each litter, with the concomitant duty to make sure that these tiny Morkies will find good homes with good owners.

Understanding Designer Dog Crossbreeds

A Morkie is just one of the many types of Designer Cross Breeds now growing in popularity today. You can typically recognize them by the hybrid of the names of their parents: a Morkie, for instance, is a combination of Maltese and Yorkie, and is also sometimes called Maltiyork, Malkie, Yorkiemalt, Yortese, or Yorktese. Other examples include the Goldendoodle (Golden Retriever and Poodle), a Bagle Hound (Basset Hound and Beagle), or a Malti-Pug (Maltese and Poodle). But the variations are literally infinite. As long as you bring together two different dog breeds, and name their offspring with a mash-up of their parents' names, you can have the makings of a designer crossbreed dog.

But what, you may ask, is the difference between a designer crossbreed and a regular old mutt? After all, it isn't like crossbreeding has never been heard of before. The resulting dogs are usually referred to as mutts, which is one way of saying they lack purebred status.

The difference, according to breeders of designer dog breeds, is in a way the same: designer dogs are bred from purebreds, with well-documented ancestry, whereas nobody knows for sure what parents mutts came from. So in a way, there is still some effort at preserving purebred characteristics - the desired characteristics of each breed, including the avoidance of any congenital or genetic illnesses or health conditions . It is just that this time, the genes are being mixed with another purebred mix in order to come up with a unique genetic pool, and hopefully one that preserves the desired characteristics from both parents. To be more precise about it, these designer dogs are more accurately referred to as "first generation hybrid dogs." Later on, these first generation hybrids can be crossed with another first generation hybrid, or another purebred. Their offpsring crossed together can result in second to third generations of hybrid dogs.

Obviously, crossbreeding can be risky in that you don't know what precisely what you're going to get. This is one of the advantages of having purebred dogs: you know what to expect and can therefore plan ahead for the dog's care throughout its entire life. You also have a good idea of the dog's temperament, their unique quirks and traits, and their specific needs in terms of care, nutrition, exercise, training, and even grooming.

The responsibilities for cross-breeding dogs are, therefore, also greater. You cannot simply abandon or discard a puppy that didn't turn out as you expected it to. Unlike purebreds, there are no guarantees and low foreseeability when it comes to crossbreeding. For a Morkie, there are still a lot of unknowns about this new breed. A Morkie can lean more towards its Maltese parent or its

Yorkie parent, and their particulare care must be adjusted to accommodate the possible inherited genetic traits from both parents. This would necessarily include the possibility of congenital health conditions that both original breeds are prone to.

One final word of caution to potential crossbreeders is to do their research. You must know each breed you are crossing very well before you attempt to breed them. Do your research so that you know the temperament and care requirements for both breeds, and make sure that both are at least compatible with the kind of crossbreed you are aiming for. If there is anything about either breed that is not a match for the kind of dog you had in mind, then you should probably avoid that cross and look at the possibility of using another breed. Again, do your research! And needless to say, it is important that both parents are as healthy as possible, with as little chance of passing on genetic conditions to their crossbreed offpsring.

Advantages and Disadvantages of Cross Breeding

So you've decided you'd like to try crossbreeding to produce a Morkie? Before you do so, here are some potential advantages and disadvantages of crossbreeding that you might want to consider before you take the plunge:

Advantages of Crossbreeding:

- It is said that designer breeds have hybrid vigor - or extra strength that comes from their double purebred pedigree. This is because - aside from the fact that you are bringing together two completely healthy purebreds, the possible genetic defects that come from inbreeding are also eliminated. You are widening the gene pool, so to speak, thus allowing for a greater possible resistance to certain illnesses or conditions.

- Many designer dogs have a more even temperament. After all, this is one of the main purposes for which they are bred: their capacity live alongside their owners' intended lifestyle: thus, a quiet, calm and gentle dog with low maintenance and exercise needs is usually the most sought after. The parents' breeds are chosen for this very reason, and many designer dogs do seem to live up to this ideal: they are small or miniature dogs that require little space and little exercise, and yet they are usually quite gentle and even-tempered. The Morkie is one example of a designer crossbreed dog that is already quite popular for being gentle, playful and loyal to its owners, while also a quiet and calm breed.

- Aside from the seemingly infinite variety of crossbreeds to choose from, designer dogs are also bred for their appearance. The results are usually very adorable and unique-looking dogs that are certainly beautiful and endearing to look at. Perhaps the designation of "designer" dog is not an accident, as surely their unique appearance is one factor that contributes to their comparatively high cost. Designer dogs, these days, have certainly gotten very useful PR from being seen alongside celebrities who carry them along as a kind of fashion statement. Crossbreeding is therefore an advantage for those who seek unique dogs with an adorable or attractive look.

- Designer dogs are the modern version of the same kind of crossbreeding that resulted in today's purebreds. If the crossbreeding of any one designer dog is carried on responsibly over several generations of hybrids, your crossbreed may someday become the original parents of a future dog breed. This requires commitment, cooperation among breeders, and a genuine desire to improve the breed. But if successful, it can also be very satisfying and worthwhile.

Disadvantages of Crossbreeding:

- In terms of cost, crossbreeding can be prohibitive. Not only are you working with two purebreeds, but designer dogs are priced quite high. That means you might find yourself having more than a little difficulty in selling the puppies among prospective owners who regard crossbreeds with more than a little suspicion, or are at least unwilling to shell out the extra cost for a designer dog.

- Even the most reputable purebred dog breeders will tell you that there is no such thing as a 100 % health guarantee when it comes to breeding dogs - no matter how many health checks you give your breeding pair. There is always a possibility that a certain illness or condition can pop up in some offspring - particularly those canine illnesses that we know little to nothing about. For crossbreeds, the risk is doubly greater because each litter is at risk for potential health conditions from two different breeds.

- While the general intention of crossbreeders is to come up with crossbreeds that combine desired characteristics of two different breeds, given the lack of a guarantee and the low level of predictability as to what the offsprings will turn out to be, it is always a distinct possibility that the new puppies might actually turn out to possess all the characteristics you *did not* want. You may not like, for instance, a Morkie with a stubborn streak, with a coat type and color you did not like, a penchant for destroying things, and one that yaps all night, disturbing the neighbors and your own family - but it is possible.

- One of the dangers of crossbreeding may lie in the breeding process itself. That is, there is a potential for high risk deliveries of crossbreed offsprings. This is particularly true in attempts to crossbreed different-sized breeds, where one is larger than the other. A smaller female may have labor difficulties for puppies larger than the usual newborns of her own breed, and may thus require a C-section for a safe birth.

- It may just turn out that crossbreeding is simply another passing fad, especially with some of the more bizarre crossbreed mixes. While the popularity and demand for unique designer dogs has increased, there has, unfortunately, also been an increase in unwanted stray crossbreeds that are unable to find a good home. Whether you decide to breed purebred dogs or to create a crossbreed, the responsibility of a breeder in caring for the puppies up until they find a new home with good owners - some may some the responsibility is for the puppies' entire lifetime - is still the same.

Basic Dog Breeding Information

Producing a Morkie can be done in several different ways. You can cross:

- A purebred Maltese and a purebred Yorkshire Terrier to produce a first generation Morkie
- A first generation Morkie with a purebred Maltese
- A first generation Morkie with a purebed Yorkshire Terrier
- A first generation Morkie with another first generation Morkie to produce a second generation Morkie

In all of the above instances, responsible breeding behooves you to breed only for the improvement of the breed - which means that you should breed only those dogs that have been health-checked, and ideally, those that display the best characteristics of the breed. Be discerning, be careful, do your research, consult with a veterinarian, consult with breeders of both purebreeds and crossbreeds, ask all the questions you need to ask and address all your doubts before you actually start breeding. Once you have satisfied yourself on all these points - including the advisability of crossbreeding in the first place, the next thing you should turn your attention to is the breeding process itself.

Make a careful selection of the prospective parents, keeping in mind the target crossbreed offspring you are attempting to create. Ask yourself why you are doing this, and whether you are ready to take on the responsibility for the puppies once they are conceived, up until they are placed with good homes and responsible owners. Be prepared to bear the financial burden of their care, including that of the mother from pregnancy until lactation, as well as the care, the weaning and the early vaccinations of the puppies.

Once you have satisfied yourself that you are fully prepared to crossbreed for a Morkie, and have made a careful selection of the prospective parents, it is time to turn your attention to the breeding process itself.

The breeding of most dogs do follow certain uniform principles: a female dog should not be bred during their time of first heat because they are too immature for the stress and responsibility of pregnancy. For toy breeds like Maltese, Yorkshire and Morkies, the age of first heat usually happens at around 6 months of age, though the precise age can vary considerably between individual dogs. For others, it can happen earlier or much later. Breeders generally advise waiting until after the third or fourth heat before you breed your toy dog - or not until they are two years of age. Some also recommend waiting until the stud is also of this age, since it also does take some maturity in both parents for the mating process to proceed smoothly and without incident.

You will recognize when the female is in heat when their vulva swells. There is also a bloody vaginal discharge. This signals the first stage of the female cycle, or the proestrus. This stage usually lasts for about nine days. The female will not allow breeding at this time, but it may be advisable for some socialization to take place between the dam and the stud. Thus, you will need to have the capacity to house and to take care of both the male and the female during this time up until mating - or for about two weeks.

Once the female enters the second stage, or estrus, the discharge becomes lighter in color. She will be ovulating at this stage, and will now be ready to accept the male. You might even be able to recognize this stage by behavioral signs in the female: a flirtatious kind of approach to the male, including a lifting of the tail to the side - called "flagging." Most experts agree that the most fertile period for dogs is during the 12th to 14th day after the bleeding began. Once mating is successful, it can be repeated at least once a day for the next two or three days - or until the female stops accepting the male. This is to help ensure a successful pregnancy.

The mating process itself is pretty straightforward. The male mounts the female from behind, and there will be penetration and ejaculation after a series of rapid pelvic thrusts. They will not separate for another 10 to 30 minutes, and the male will usually move until they are standing rear to rear. This is what is known as a tie, and is caused by the swelling of the male's penis. They will separate naturally after some time, so it is not advisable to try to force them to separate as this may cause injury and trauma to either or both dogs.

After estrus, the female will enter a stage called diestrus, and may last for about 60 to 90 days. Some females will manifest signs of false pregnancy during this time. That is why it is advisable to confirm pregnancy only after 28 days - which a veterinarian can do through either abdominal palpitations, ultrasound, or x-rays. If breeding is successful and pregnancy confirmed, then it is time for you to settle down to take care of the pregnant mother.

Dog Pregnancy Basics

A dog's gestation period lasts approximately 63 days. It is best for you to consult with your veterinarian regarding the special care you would be taking of the pregnant mother during this time - including recommendations for diet and exercise regimens. Generally, however, her daily intake should be gradually increased as she begins to gain weight, and her exercise should also be moderated during this time. Towards the end of the pregnancy, she should be eating anywhere from 20 to 50 percent more than her regular diet. Be careful - especially with miniature or toy breeds - that these diet changes should be implemented slowly and gradually during the last five weeks of pregnancy. To better accustom her small size to the bigger diet portions, you could apportion her food into several small meals each day. Don't forget to consult with your veterinarian regarding any necessary nutrients she may be needing during her pregnancy.

You should also begin to accustom her to her whelping box during this time. This should be roomy enough to accommodate her and her prospective litter, with room enough for them to move, and raised sides to provide security to the puppies. Many breeders choose to line this with newspaper which they can change as needed. Keep this box in a secure, private place that is free from drafts or cold air. Gradually, as her whelping time approaches, you will find her seeking the comfort of her whelping box more and more.

Signs that your pregnant dog is about ready to give birth include a sudden drop in temperature - from 102.5 to about 99 degrees. The first stage of labor should start within the next 24 hours. You should already make arrangements to be present during the entire birthing process - ready to assist should there be a need for your intervention. Also keep your vet's phone number and the number of the nearest emergency clinic handy so that you can make a call should there be any troubles or difficulties during whelping.

You will notice her panting and straining right before each puppy is about to be born. There will be abdominal contractions, the cervix will dilate, and each puppy will come one after another - usually at intervals of about ten to thirty minutes each.

Puppies will come with their own placenta. This will break naturally once they puppies are born, but if it doesn't, the mother should tear at this and at the umbilical cord, after which she will proceed to lick at the puppy's face and nostrils to stimulate breathing. First time mothers may not know to do this at first. You can carefully tear at the placenta yourself to free the pup, using a moist towel to wipe at its nose and mouth to clear the airways. Unwaxed dental floss can be used to sever the umbilical cord, and the application of iodine on the cut ends to prevent infection. Once the mother sees what is expected of her, she will usually step in and do these things herself.

Puppies should each come with their own placenta, so make sure to count each as they come out. A missing placenta means that it might have been left inside the mother - which could lead to complications further on. In such instances, you should call your veterinarian. Also remember that while it takes some time for each puppy to come, labor should never exceed two hours. If the mother has been straining for more than an hour with no pup in sight, again, you should call your veterinarian.

In the resting period between each puppy's birth, you can assist the newborn pups to nurse from their mother.

This first milk - also called the colostrum, is necessary for the newborn pups. It provides them with their mother's immunity, and is very important because newborn pups have - as yet - no immune system to speak of. Though it might be good to remember that they will only be getting immunity against diseases for which their mother had received the appropriate vaccinations.

Throughout this entire process, make sure to take good care of the whelping mother - provide her with a drinking bowl in case she gets thirsty. She will likely not have an appetite during this time. More importantly, reassure her with your presence and soft, soothing words.

The following instances also warrant an immediate phone call to your veterinarian or to emergency services:

- Contractions lasting for more than 45 minutes with no puppy being born
- The passing of a dark green or bloody fluid before the first puppy is born (this is considered normal after the birth of the first puppy)
- Signs of extreme pain or painful contractions
- No signs of labor or whelping even after the 64th day after the last mating

Special care should still be taken of the mother even after whelping. She will be lactating and nursing the puppies during this time - which means that she will need all the nutrients they can get. Consult with your veterinarian on the recommended diet for a lactating dam to help support her during this demanding time. Also watch out for the possible onset of eclampsia, which causes symptoms such as whimpering, spasms and an unseady gait. This can usually be addressed by a proper diet and sufficient amounts of recommended nutrients.

Caring for and Weaning the Puppies

Puppies are helpless during the first two weeks - their eyes and ears are closed, and they will not be able to do much other than sleep and nurse. They also cannot regulate their body temperature during this time so it is necessary that they be kept in a warm, preferably private place that is free from constant interruptions and drafts. A puppy catching a chill can be a very dangerous thing.

The best thing that you can do at this time is to pay attention to each pup and to the mother. Make sure that the mother is fed well, and that her her teats are free of any abnormalities so that she could nurse her litter sufficiently. Observe the puppies - plump and healthy-looking puppies means that the mother is producing enough nourishing milk for her young ones. Keep their area clean, and change their beddings regularly because they will be defecating and urinating in the whelping box. If you notice any of the puppies seem underfed or whining constantly, it may mean that something is wrong. They should also gain weight progressively - weighing them regularly should confirm steady weight gain. If not, a veterinarian can guide you as to whether this means that you might have to supplement-feed the pups to make sure that they are all getting proper nourishment.

The puppy's eyes and ears will begin to develop at around the 10th day, though full development will still progress during the next few days. You can then have the puppies and the mother de-wormed at around the 12th day. You can begin weaning the puppies when they are around 4 weeks of age, though as with any dietary changes, this should be done gradually to avoid digestive upsets. Consult with your veterinarian regarding this. Many breeders opt for a mixture of puppy food soaked in milk or broth to supplement their mother's milk to start with, gradually increasing the proportions over the next couple of weeks. Generally, puppies should be fully weaned at 8 weeks.

Socialization should already have started at this time. It begins, of course, with the pup's relationship with his mother and his siblings. But you will be there, too - and gentle, daily handling or your simple presence will accustom him to the presence of a human. Socialization should take place as early as possible so that newborn dogs will grow accustomed to living alongside humans. Once they are comfortable with being away from their mother for long periods of time, and are already fully weaned, they may be ready to be brought home by their new owners.

Chapter Nine: Keeping Your Morkie Dog Healthy

Morkies can be a fragile and delicate breed - in terms of their physical structure. Being small dogs, rough games are not really recommended. But aside from their physical aptitude, like any other dog breed, a combination of good care and good genes can make for a healthy Morkie with a relatively long life span. If you have any questions regarding their health issues, the most efficient thing to do is to inquire about the health and medical history of both parents. Any genetic or inherited disorders can usually be traced to illnesses or conditions that may have been present in one or both parents. Like with any crossbreed, looking into the potential health conditions of the breeds of both parents is also advised.

It is always good to remember that, being a relatively new breed that is still on its way to official recognition by various kennel clubs all over the world, it cannot be said with any amount of certainty that Morkies as a breed are prone to developing certain health conditions. There are some common health problems, however, that have been found to affect some Morkie Dogs. Information regarding these are provided below.

Common Health Problems Affecting Morkie Dogs

- **Collapsed Trachea**
- **Reverse Sneezing**
- **Cataracts**
- **Medial Patellar Luxation**
- **Hydrocephalus**
- **Chronic Valvular Heart Disease**
- **Kidney Failure**
- **Glaucoma**

Collapsed Trachea

This is a genetic condition more commonly found among Yorkies, and it can affect both sexes. This happens when some of the rings of cartilage that make up the windpipe collapse, creating an airway obstruction in the trachea or windpipe.

It is theorized that a general weakness in the cartilage of the tracheal rings is a predisposing condition. The collapse of the cartilage itself may be precipitated by obesity, excitement, drinking or eating, irritants such as smoke or dust, exercise, and hot and humid weather.

Signs and symptoms of this condition include labored breathing, a bluish tinge to the gums, and a characteristic honking cough that results from air being squeezed through the trachea. It can manifest at any age, though mostly at around six or seven years. The difficulty here is that surgery, which is recommended for advanced cases of tracheal collapse, becomes more precarious for dogs that are older than six years.

Diagnosis is done through radiographs and fluoroscopy, although the honking cough is considered highly suggestive. Treatment may be done with cough suppressants and antibiotics, with recommendations for weight loss therapy for obese dogs. Surgery - which is a very specialized kind for this condition - is reserved mostly for very severe cases.

For the owner of a Morkie with diagnosed tracheal collapse, there are various things you can do to ease your pet's condition. Aside from a careful weight loss regimen for obese dogs, you can avoid respiratory irritants such as dust or smoke, and switch to a harness instead of a collar. The goal is to relieve respiratory stress as much as possible.

Reverse Sneezing

Reverse Sneezing is more commonly seen among the tinier dog breeds. The good news is that it isn't harmful in and of itself, unless accompanied by other telling symptoms, though it can be rather alarming for pet owners having to contend with their dogs going through the gross symptoms of this condition.

Sometimes called Pharyngeal Gag Reflex or Paroxysmal Respiration, it is caused by a spasm in the soft palate and laryngeal area which triggers a reverse sneeze - literally, because instead of expelling air like in a sneeze, the result is a heavy gasping inward of air.

Dogs extend their neck during a reverse sneeze, and they "sneeze" with a kind of loud, grunting or honking sound. Their eyes may stick out and their chests expand, mostly because they are seeking to get enough air. It can be very frightening when it happens, but it usually only lasts for a few minutes, and ends on its own, even without any intervention. There are usually no lasting effects on the dog's overall health.

It is theorized that allergies may cause reverse sneezing, and can be triggered by a wide variety of irritants. Other possible causes are excitability, rapid drinking or eating, or pulling on leashes. Some respiratory conditions may also set off episodes of reverse sneezing.

Treatment depends on the cause. If it is found to be caused by allergies, removal of the trigger is recommended, along with prescribed antihistamines in cases of exposure. During the episode itself, the owner may try a gentle massage on the throat to help relieve the symptom, or some also try covering the dog's nostrils to help the dog swallow, thus clearing the obstruction. Otherwise, you can try depressing the tongue to help the air move through the nasal passage.

While Reverse Sneezing is generally harmless, if it occurs frequently or seems severe, always seek your veterinarian's professional opinion in case it is a symptom of a more severe underlying cause. It may be helpful to keep records of the circumstances of each episode - such as what circumstances preceded it, how long it lasted, or what time of day and environmental factors were prevalent during each occurrence. You may also want to take a video to show your vet later on.

Cataracts

Cataracts are the result of a disruption in the normal arrangement of the lens fibers in the eyes, resulting in a loss of transparency and reduction of vision. The more common symptom is a cloudy white appearance in the lens of the eye. It can be either genetic or caused by other factors such as trauma or injury, or an illness such as diabetes. Thus, it can manifest at any age. For older dogs, or dogs over six years of age, what may appear as cataracts may actually be nuclear sclerosis, which doesn't actually have any effect on the dog's vision.

Proper diagnosis, therefore, is important - especially when it comes to treatment. Cataracts are treated with surgery, while if cataract formation is the result of an illness, such as diabetes, for example, then treatment of the underlying illness is more appropriate.

Watch out for possible signs of vision loss, such as a tendency to bump into walls or furniture, or a certain timidity or caution in walking or playing. If untreated, a cataract may slip from where it is held in place, thus floating freely in the eye where it may block fluid drainage and cause more serious conditions such as glaucoma and thereafter, blindness. On the other hand, the cataract may also dissolve on its own, causing painful eye inflammation.

The prognosis for surgical treatment of cataracts is generally good, so early detection and early treatment is best.

Medial Patellar Luxation

This is the canine version of a "trick knee," and happens when the knee cap, also called the patella, luxates or slips from the groove where it rides over the femur, or the large bone of the thigh. More commonly, the patella slips to the inside of the knee, though sometimes it can also slip to the outside of the knee. This condition may affect one or both of your pet's knees.

This is a genetic condition that is more common among smaller dogs, and may be caused by a trochlear groove that is too shallow, causing the patella to luxate. In some instances, the ligament keeping the patella in place may be overstretched or weak. Though there have also been instances when this condition has been caused by injury or trauma.

You can recognize this condition when your Morkie's legs and knees seem to "lock up" as it walks, or a kind of skipping gait. You may see your Morkie sort of shake this off, or extend their legs before regaining full function once again. But if it happens again, it is best to bring him to your veterinarian for proper diagnosis and treatment. An x-ray can confirm whether or not it is Medial Patellar Luxation.

Treatment depends on severity. Once again, early detection and immediate treatment is best. There are four recognized grades of Medial Patellar Luxation, Grade I being the less severe, and Grade IV the most severe. While Grade I can be treated with a massage when the leg is fully extended, Grades II to IV require surgical correction, with lateral collateral ligament reinforcement being the less intrusive and safer surgical option. If untreated, the more severe cases may later lead on to irreversible arthritis.

Hydrocephalus

Hydrocephalus is sometimes called "water in the brain," which is a pretty literal definition of what happens in this condition. Once there is an excess of cerebrospinal fluid (CSF), it can leak inside the skull causing brain swelling. The increased pressure within the skull can press on the brain tisses, leading to intercranial pressure, sometimes brain damage, and even death.

Hydrocephalus can either be genetic or acquired. It is found to be more common in smaller, or miniature and toy breed dogs. If genetic, it can be identified with a dome-shaped skull, a large fontanel, and eyes that appear to gaze down. It can also manifest in abnormal walking, circling or falling over on the side, and a certain inability to learn basic commands. Acquired hydrocephalus, on the other hand, may be caused by infection or tumors. In addition to the symptoms mentioned above, the Morkie may also display listlessness, pacing, seizures, and "head pressing" or pressing the head against something solid. Other possible symptoms include hyperexcitability, aggression, stunted growth, respiratory difficulties, changes in stride, gaint, stance or posture, abnormal eye positions, vision abnormalities, disorientation, stupor, or coma.

Treatment necessarily involves the reduction of CSF production. If caught early, this can be done with prescribed corticosteroids to help reduce CSF production and inflammation. The more severe cases may also include anti-seizure medications.

Some veterinary and specialty hospitals also offer surgery that uses a tube to open spaces in the brain, shunting the CSF to the abdomen or other locations in the body. This is a pretty complicated procedure, though success rates are reportedly quite high. If the hydrocephalus is acquired, then treatment of the underlying cause is recommended. Prognosis in general depends on various factors, but for cases congenital cases of hydrocephalus, the outlook is usually quite poor. Selective breeding of healthy Morkies is, therefore, important. Morkies diagnosed with, or those that have a family history of congenital hydrocephalus, should not be bred.

Chronic Degenerative Heart Valve Disease

Known as CVD for short, this condition is also referred to as endocardiosis, and is caused by a thickening of a heart valve - in most cases of the mitral heart valve in the left ventricle. This valve admits oxygenated blood into the heart, while generating pressure and blood flow to supply the body with oxygenated blood when it contracts. When CVD happens, blood can leak back into the left atrial chamber whenever the valve contracts. The severity of this condition depends on how severe the leakage is.

Some of the more initial symptoms include a heart murmur, which is caused by the turbulent blood flow in the heart. This can usually be detected with a stethoscope, and warrants further examination. Other symptoms include coughing, gagging, difficulty breathing, fainting, and exercise intolerance. An echocardiogram can confirm the presence of CVD, by providing an ultrasound study of the heart.

This is a condition that may begin to develop early on in a dog's life, though it is not apparent until years later. Predisposing genetic conditions may thus actually be present throughout a dog's life.

Possible treatment includes prescriped medication and a salt-restricted diet, though this is mainly to ease the symptoms, and is thus dependent on individual cases.

Surgery may also be possible, but open-heart surgery for dogs is not a popular choice because of its cost and the difficulty of the procedure.

Kidney Failure

Kidney failure affects many dogs and cats, and in many instances, it is simply the result of old age and the gradual wear and tear of the kidneys. Sometimes though, it may be caused by infection, cancer, parasites, trauma, or a toxic reaction to certain substances. In any case, the most common symptoms are an increase in urine and in water consumption. Other symptoms include a decrease in appetite, weight loss, lethargy, diarrhea, and a poor hair or coat condition.

Diagnosis is done by blood tests, urinalysis, and a blood count to check for anemia and possible infection. The kidneys work by cleaning the blood of excess salts and water. Once the kidneys begin to fail, there will be an accumulation of waste in the body, leading to excess thirst and urination. In more severe cases, there can be weight loss and anemia. Treatment options can range from specialized diets, fluid therapy, and antibiotics to prevent infection. Supplements may be given to restore electrolyte and phosphorous levels. Some veterinary clinics also offer kidney dialysis and kidney transplants. Depending on the treatment and how their body responds, some dogs may live for months or years after being diagnosed with CRF.

Glaucoma

Glaucoma happens when there is an elevated pressure from fluid buildup inside the eye. This can cause retinal damage and, over time, blindness. This can be a painful condition for your dog, so early detection and treatment is important. When caught early, treatment by medication to decrease intraocular pressure may still be possible. If medication is not effective, surgery may also be offered as an option. If neither medication or surgery works, the eye may have to be removed. Though a drastic procedure, the latter option might at least remove the source of the severe and chronic pain that comes with severe glaucoma.

It is therefore important that your dog has regular veterinary checkups that include eye examinations. Some symptoms can be seen in the eyes, such as redness, cloudiness, abnormal discharges, bulging eyes, or dilated pupils. There may also be extreme sensitivity where they dislike being petted near the eyes, avoidance or sensitivity to light, rubbing at the eyes or the face, or a tendency to squint. There may also be some behavioral symptoms, which can include lethargy, stumbling or bumping into things, excessive barking, lethargy, agitation, disorientation, or visible signs of pain.

Preventing Illness with Vaccinations

There are some standard vaccination schedules that apply to most dog breeds, though this varies considerably depending on your location and the current state of diseases in your region. Be sure to consult with your veterinarian regarding the recommended vaccinations and the frequency and dosage of each.

It may also be worthwhile to remember that unlike larger dog breeds, miniature or toy breeds may not be able to handle mutiple vaccinations at too early an age. Some recommend waiting until at least seven weeks before the first vaccination for a Morkie, which are a pretty fragile and delicate breed. Since vaccines work by introducing dead versions of a certain disease to stimulate the body's immune sytem against that disease, the body's immune system has to be mature enough to cope with the introduction of these foreign threats.

Some also claim that introducing combination vaccines at the same time may even overload the dog's immune system. And yet, if a puppy is at high risk of exposure to regional incidence of certain diseases, it might be said that an earlier vaccination is preferable. Amidst these conflicting information, and the variations of your dog's breed, weight, and the regional incidence of diseases, recommended vaccination schedules can certainly vary. Don't hesitate to gather whatever information you will need to arrive at a decision regarding your Morkie's vaccination: read, ask questions, discuss it with your veterinarian, don't be afraid to voice your concerns, and use your best judgment.

And yet certain core vaccinations are certainly necessary. Despite the number of health conditions - whether congenital or acquired - to which Morkies are prone to, the state of veterinary medicine is in a continual state of progress and development. Many of the diseases once considered fatal to dogs are now vaccinated against, and that is why vaccines are important. These would include some of what are considered core vaccines: for canine distemper, parvovirus, hepatitis, and rabies. Non-core vaccines, on the other hand, include measles, adenovirus, parainfluenza, bordetella, coronavirus, lyme disease, and leptospirosis.

The following table shows a standard dog vaccination schedule, showing recommended administrations of core and non-core vaccines:

Age	Core (Recommended)	Non-Core
6-8 weeks	Distemper, Hepatitis, Parainfluenza, Parvovirus	Bordetella
10-12 weeks	Distemper, Hepatitis, Leptospirosis, Parainfluenza, Parvovirus	Coronavirus
12-16 weeks	Distemper, Hepatitis, Leptospiros, Parainfluenza, Parvovirus, Rabies	Lyme Disease
1 year	Distemper, Hepatitis, Leptospiros, Parainfluenza, Parvovirus, Rabies	Bordetella, Coronavirus, Lyme Disease

Again, while it seems a simple thing to make sure that your dog gets all the vaccines he needs, the recent influx of information regarding possible adverse reactions to too much and too soon administration of vaccines should give us pause. Exercise due caution by being discerning and staying as informed as possible, and discuss your concerns with your veterinarian. It is probably a good idea, however, to make sure that your Morkie at least gets a good dose of the core vaccines at a reasonable age: at around 7-8 weeks.

Morkie Care Sheet

1.) Basic Havanese Information

Pedigree: Maltese, Yorkshire Terrier

AKC Group: not applicable

Types: not applicable

Breed Size: small

Height: 6 - 8 inches

Weight: 4 - 12 lbs.

Coat Length and Texture: Long and soft, fine and straight

Color: black, brown, tan or white

Appearance: Not standard

Temperament: active and playful, quite needy and form strong attachments to their owners; they can be excitable, energetic, and loyal, with a streak of stubbornness

Strangers: suspicious of strangers and will bark to alert of unusual sounds

Other Dogs: normally friendly with other dogs they have been brought up with

Other Pets: normally friendly with other pets that they have been brought up with

Training: intelligent and smart, but can be difficult; training should begin as early as possible

Exercise Needs: moderate; a few short walks each day with occasional play time

Health Conditions: eye, ear and oral regions: collapsed trachea, reverse sneezing, tracheal collapse, cataracts, medial patellar luxation, hydrocephalus, chronic valvular heart disease, kidney failure, glaucoma

Lifespan: average 10 to 13 years

2.) Habitat Requirements

Recommended Accessories: crate, dog bed, food/water dishes, treats, toys, collar, leash, identification tag, harness, grooming supplies

Collar and Harness: sized by weight

Grooming Supplies: *slicker, bristle or steel pin brush, 2-in-1 comb, shedding blade, liquid detangler or baby oil*

Grooming Frequency: moderate to high

Energy Level: moderately active and playful

Exercise Requirements: about 20-40 minutes of exercise per day

Crate: highly recommended

Crate Size: just large enough for dog to lie down and turn around comfortably

Crate Extras: lined with blanket or plush pet bed

Food/Water: stainless steel or ceramic bowls, clean daily

Toys: start with an assortment, see what the dog likes; include some mentally stimulating toys

Exercise Ideas: short walks, ball games

3.) Nutritional Needs

Nutritional Needs: water, protein, carbohydrate, fats, vitamins, minerals

RER: *30(body weight in kilograms) + 70*

Calorie Needs: varies by age, weight, and activity level; RER modified with activity level

Amount to Feed: 3 small meals per day

Important Ingredients: fresh animal protein (chicken, beef, lamb, turkey, eggs), digestible carbohydrates (rice, oats, barley), animal fats

Important Minerals: calcium, phosphorus, potassium, magnesium, iron, copper and manganese

Important Vitamins: Vitamin A, Vitamin A, Vitamin B-12, Vitamin D, Vitamin C

Look For: AAFCO statement of nutritional adequacy; protein at top of ingredients list; no artificial flavors, dyes, preservatives

4.) Breeding Information

Age of First Heat: around 6 months, sometimes earlier or later

Heat (Estrus) Cycle: 14 to 21 days

Frequency: twice a year, every 6 to 7 months

Greatest Fertility: 11 to 15 days into the cycle

Gestation Period: 59 to 63 days

Pregnancy Detection: possible after 21 days, best to wait 28-30 days before exam

Feeding Pregnant Dogs: maintain normal diet until week 5 or 6 then slightly increase rations by 20 to 50 percent for the last five weeks

Signs of Labor: body temperature drops below normal 100° to 102°F (37.7° to 38.8°C), may be as low as 98°F (36.6°C); dog begins nesting in a dark, quiet place

Contractions: *ten to thirty minutes, in waves of an hour or so each time*

Whelping: may last anywhere from a few hours to half a day or more

Puppies: born with eyes and ears closed; eyes open at 3 weeks, teeth develop at 10 weeks

Litter Size: average 3-5 puppies

Size at Birth: 4-5 oz.

Weaning: supplement with controlled portions of moistened puppy food at 3-5 weeks, with water freely available, fully weaned at 5-6 weeks

Socialization: start as early as possible to prevent puppies from being nervous as an adult, preferably before 14-16 weeks of age

Index

U

V

W

X

Y

Photo Credits

Cover Photo by BluBb mADe via Wikimedia Commons. <https://commons.wikimedia.org/wiki/File:Yorkshire_Malt eser_Mix.jpg>

Page 1 Photo by Cachang via Wikimedia Commons. <https://commons.wikimedia.org/wiki/File:Morkie_maltes e_body.jpg>

Page 9 Photo by Chelsearock via Wikimedia Commons. <https://commons.wikimedia.org/wiki/File:Khloe.jpg>

Page 15 Photo by Kr0n05931 via Wikimedia Commons. <https://commons.wikimedia.org/wiki/File:Morkie_puppy _maltese-like.png>

Page 25 Photo by Chealsearock via Wikimedia Commons. <https://commons.wikimedia.org/wiki/File:KMorkie.jpg>

Page 31 Photo by David Martin :: Suki_:: <http://sukiweb.openphoto.net/gallery/> via openphoto.net. <http://openphoto.net/gallery/image/view/7277>

Page 37 Photo by Jordan Miller. <http://helloandhi.openphoto.net/gallery/> via openphoto.net. <http://openphoto.net/gallery/image/view/21627>

Page 47 Photo by Michael Jastremski.
<http://mike.openphoto.net/gallery/> via openphoto.net.
<http://openphoto.net/gallery/image/view/5343>

Page 55 Photo by Chelsearock via Wikimedia Commons.
<https://commons.wikimedia.org/wiki/File:MorkieWalk.JP
G>

Page 63 Photo by Kr0n05931 via Wikimedia Commons.
<https://commons.wikimedia.org/wiki/File:Morkies-1yr-
old-same-litter.JPG>

Page 83 Photo by Barbara Cooper.
<http://bcoop.openphoto.net/gallery/> via openphoto.net.
<http://openphoto.net/gallery/image/view/21586>

Page 99 Photo by Ilmionome (Satyricon86) via Wikimedia
Commons.
<https://commons.wikimedia.org/wiki/File:Niki-morkie-
designer-dog.jpg>

References

"10 Things You Should Know Before Buying a Morkie." puppytoob.com. <http://puppytoob.com/dog-breeds/10-things-know-buying-morkie/>

"5 Easy Techniques to Grooming Morkie Dogs." My Puppy Blog. <https://kinleex3.wordpress.com/2014/01/11/5-easy-techniques-to-grooming-morkie-dogs/>

"A Dog's Menstrual (Heat) Cycle." PetWave. <http://www.petwave.com/Dogs/Basics/Breeding/Heat.aspx>

"Advantages and Disadvantages of Cross Breeding Dogs." love to know <http://dogs.lovetoknow.com/dog-breeding-pregnancy/advantages-disadvantages-cross-breeding-dogs>

"AKC Rescue Network." <AKC. http://www.akc.org/dog-breeds/rescue-network/>

"Best Puppy Food for Your Morkie." Lonestar66. <http://thepugglehouse.com/best-puppy-food-for-your-morkie/>

"Cataracts in Dogs." Veterinary & Aquatic Services Department, Drs. Foster & Smith. <http://www.peteducation.com/article.cfm?c=2+2092&aid=407>

"Breeding for Dog Owners - Caring for Newborn Puppies."
VCA. <http://www.vcahospitals.com/main/pet-health-
information/article/animal-health/breeding-for-dog-
owners-caring-for-newborn-puppies/488>

"Canine Nutrition Basics." Claudia Kawczynska.
<http://thebark.com/content/canine-nutrition-basics>

"Cataracts in Dogs." WebMd.com.
<http://pets.webmd.com/dogs/cataracts-dogs>

"Cesar Milan's Positive Dog Training Techniques."
shibashake. <https://pethelpful.com/dogs/Cesar-Milan-
Dog-Training-the-Dog-Whisperer>

"Choosing a Puppy." apdt.co.uk.
<http://www.apdt.co.uk/dog-owners/choosing-a-puppy>

"Chronic Degenerative Heart Valve Disease in Dogs."
Vermont Veterinary Cardiology Services.
<http://www.vermontveterinarycardiology.com/index.php
/for-cardiologists/unusual-veterinary-cardiology-
cases?id=211>

"Chronic Valvular Heart Disease in Dogs." PetPlace.com
Veterinarians.
<http://www.petplace.com/article/dogs/diseases-
conditions-of-dogs/heart-blood-vessels/chronic-valvular-
heart-disease-in-dogs>

"Designer Dogs (Hybrid Dogs). dogbreedinfo.com.
<http://www.dogbreedinfo.com/designerdogs.htm>

"Dog Crossbreed." Wikipedia. <https://en.wikipedia.org/wiki/Dog_crossbreed#Designer_dogs>

"Dog Grooming Supplies." Elvis Yorkshire Terrier. <http://www.elvisyorkshireterrier.com/yorkie-grooming-supplies.php>

"Dog Nutrition Tips." ASPCA. <http://www.aspca.org/pet-care/dog-care/dog-nutrition-tips>

"Eye Diseases." Denise Hunter. <http://www.americanmaltese.org/ama-health-information/eye-diseases>

"Feeding Toy Dogs and Other Small Breeds." Pets4Homes. <http://www.pets4homes.co.uk/pet-advice/feeding-toy-dogs-and-other-small-breeds.html>

"Feeding Your Puppy Right From the Start." Small Dog Place. <http://www.smalldogplace.com/feeding-your-puppy.html>

"Foods Toxic to Dogs."

"Glaucoma in Dogs (Fluid Buildup in Dog's Eye)." PetWave. <http://www.petwave.com/Dogs/Health/Glaucoma.aspx>

"Grooming a Maltese." you-can-do-it-grooming.com. <http://www.you-can-do-it-dog-grooming.com/groomingamaltese.html>

"Help With 2 year old Morkie." The Housebreaking Bible. <http://thehousebreakingbible.com/forum/trainers/1010-help-2-morkie.html>

"Housebreaking Morkie Puppies." GFP. <https://www.greenfieldpuppies.com/2013/06/tips-for-caring-for-your-dalmation/>

"How Much Should You Feed Your Dog?" Petfinder. <https://www.petfinder.com/dogs/dog-nutrition/how-much-to-feed-your-dog/>

"How to Care for Newborn Puppies." Ashley Bennett. <https://www.cesarsway.com/dog-care/puppies/how-to-care-for-newborn-puppies>

"How to Choose a Good Puppy (Picking The Best Puppy in a Litter)." Michele Welton. <http://www.yourpurebredpuppy.com/buying/articles/how-to-choose-a-puppy.html>

"How to Clean Your Little Dog's Ears." Swank Pets Dog Blog. <http://www.swankpets.com/blog/2007/11/how-to-clean-your-little-dogs-ears/>

"How to Groom a Morkie." The Morkie Guide. <http://www.themorkieguide.com/2016/03/how-to-groom-a-morkie-dog/>

"Hydrocephalus in Toy Breed Puppies." VCA. <http://www.vcahospitals.com/main/pet-health-

information/article/animal-health/hydrocephalus-in-toy-breed-puppies/6838>

"Hydrocephalus (Water on the Brain) in Dogs." PetWave. <http://www.petwave.com/Dogs/Health/Hydrocephalus.aspx>

"Individual Meals or Free Choice???" The Teacup & Tiny Puppy Care Guide. <http://teacup-and-tiny-puppy-care.weebly.com/feeding-schedule.html>

"Just Answer." Dog Veterinary. <http://www.justanswer.com/dog-health/5ked7-one-year-old-morkie-attempted-house-train.html>

"Kidney Disease: Causes, Signs, Diagnosis and Treatment." Veterinary & Aquatic Services, Drs. Foster & Smith. <http://www.peteducation.com/article.cfm?c=2+2114&aid=350>

"Kidney Disease in Your Dog: Chronic Renal Problems." Ron Hines DVM PhD. <http://www.2ndchance.info/kidneydog.htm>

"Knee Problems in Your Dog: Patellar Luxation - Luxating Kneecaps." Ron Hines DVM PhD. <http://www.2ndchance.info/patella.htm>

"List of Hybrid Dogs." Dog Breed Info Center. <http://www.dogbreedinfo.com/hybriddogs.htm>

"Luxating Patella." Wikipedia.
    <https://en.wikipedia.org/wiki/Luxating_patella#Diagnosis
    >

"Mixed Breed Dogs - The Pros & Cons of Choosing a
    Designer Dog or a Hybrid Dog." Regina.
    <https://dogs.thefuntimesguide.com/2011/09/designer-
    dogs.php>

"Morkie." designermixes.org.
    <http://www.designermixes.org/breed_info/444/morkie.as
    px>

"Morkie." itsdogbreeds.info.
    <http://www.itsdogbreeds.info/hybrid-dogs/morkie.html>

"Morkie." Pet Guide.com.
    <http://www.petguide.com/breeds/dog/morkie/>

"Morkie." Wikipedia.
    <https://en.wikipedia.org/wiki/Morkie>

"Morkie - Needy and Playful." dogbreedplus.com.
    <http://www.dogbreedplus.com/dog_breeds/morkie.php>

"Morkie Care Tips: What You Need to Know Before Getting
    a New Puppy." Tonya M.
    <http://morkiemadness.blogspot.com/2011/05/morkie-care-
    tips-what-you-need-to-know.html>

"Morkie Information." Great Dog Site.
    <http://www.greatdogsite.com/hybrids/details/Morkie/>

"Morkie Puppies." lovetoknow.com.
  <http://dogs.lovetoknow.com/morkie-puppies>

"Patellar Luxations." acvs.org. <https://www.acvs.org/small-
  animal/patellar-luxations>

"Responsible Breeding." AKC. <http://www.akc.org/dog-
  breeders/responsible-breeding/#mating>

"Should I Let My Morkie Sleep in Bed With Me?" The
  Morkie Guide.
  <http://www.themorkieguide.com/2016/02/morkie-sleep/>

"Socializing a New Puppy." WebMD.
  <http://pets.webmd.com/dogs/guide/socializing-new-
  puppy>

"Teeth Cleaning Tips for Your Morkie." Tonya M.
  <http://morkiemadness.blogspot.com/2014/03/teeth-
  cleaning-tips-for-your-morkie.html>

"The Annual Cost of Pet Ownership: Can You Afford a
  Furry Friend?" David Weliver.
  <http://www.moneyunder30.com/the-true-cost-of-pet-
  ownership>

"The hidden suffering of the dogs bred to be cute: Adorable
  looks. Cuddly names like Labradoodle. But the trend for
  cross-breed dogs raises disturbing questions." Louise
  Eccles and Harry Mount.
  <http://www.dailymail.co.uk/news/article-2564373/The-
  hidden-suffering-dogs-bred-cute-Adorable-looks-Cuddly-

names-like-Labradoodle-But-trend-cross-breed-dogs-raises-disturbing-questions.html>

"Tracheal Collapse in Dogs." ASPCA. <http://pets.webmd.com/dogs/tracheal-collapse-dogs>

"Tricks for Treats: 6 Awesme Tricks to Teach Your Dog Right Now." Lori Taylor. <http://iheartdogs.com/tricks-for-treats-6-awesome-tricks-to-teach-your-dog-right-now/?utm_source=IHDS-Email&utm_medium=Newsletter&utm_campaign=Newsletter_11-18-15>

"Vaccination Schedule for Dogs: What Shots Your Dog Needs and When." Wyatt Robinson. <http://dogsaholic.com/care/vaccination-schedule-for-dogs.html>

"Vaccinations." Teacup & Toy Puppies. <http://www.teacupandtoypuppies.net/vaccinations-for-puppies.html>

"Vaccines." California Pet Pharmacy. <http://www.californiapetpharmacy.com/vaccines.html>

"Week by Week from birth to weaning." Royal Canin. <http://motherandpuppies.royalcanin.co.uk/from-nursing-to-weaning/week-by-week-from-birth-to-weaning/%28week%29/1>

"What Pet Food Makers DON'T Want You To Know." Dr. Karen Becker.

<http://healthypets.mercola.com/sites/healthypets/archive/ 2010/10/21/selecting-the-best-cat-pet-and-dog-pet-food.aspx>

"Why is My Dog Gasping & Honking? It Could Be A Reverse Sneeze!" Brandy Arnold. <http://www.dogingtonpost.com/reverse-sneezing-in-dogs/>

Feeding Baby
Cynthia Cherry
978-1941070000

Axolotl
Lolly Brown
978-0989658430

Dysautonomia, POTS
Syndrome
Frederick Earlstein
978-0989658485

Degenerative Disc
Disease Explained
Frederick Earlstein
978-0989658485

Sinusitis, Hay Fever,
Allergic Rhinitis Explained
Frederick Earlstein
978-1941070024

Wicca
Riley Star
978-1941070130

Zombie Apocalypse
Rex Cutty
978-1941070154

Capybara
Lolly Brown
978-1941070062

Eels As Pets
Lolly Brown
978-1941070167

Scabies and Lice Explained
Frederick Earlstein
978-1941070017

Saltwater Fish As Pets
Lolly Brown
978-0989658461

Torticollis Explained
Frederick Earlstein
978-1941070055

Kennel Cough
Lolly Brown
978-0989658409

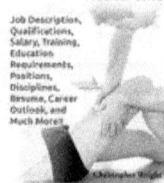

Physiotherapist, Physical
Therapist
Christopher Wright
978-0989658492

Rats, Mice, and Dormice
As Pets
Lolly Brown
978-1941070079

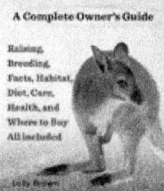

Wallaby and Wallaroo Care
Lolly Brown
978-1941070031

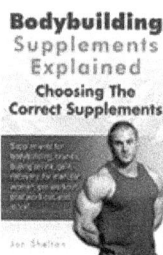

Bodybuilding Supplements
Explained
Jon Shelton
978-1941070239

Demonology
Riley Star
978-19401070314

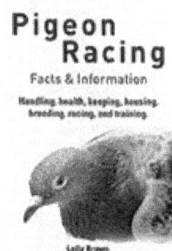

Pigeon Racing
Lolly Brown
978-1941070307

Dwarf Hamster
Lolly Brown
978-1941070390

Cryptozoology
Rex Cutty
978-1941070406

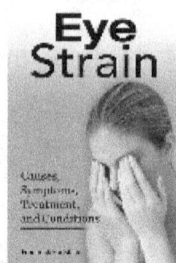

Eye Strain
Frederick Earlstein
978-1941070369

Inez The Miniature Elephant
Asher Ray
978-1941070353

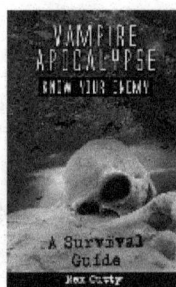

Vampire Apocalypse
Rex Cutty
978-1941070321

www.ingramcontent.com/pod-product-compliance
Lightning Source LLC
LaVergne TN
LVHW051644080426
835511LV00016B/2479